Peacef

~

A 15-step journey
of gentle practices and bodywork
towards peace and love

~

Tommaso Palumbo

First published 2006 in the UK by Phemiology Press

Phemiology Press
School of Integrated Person Care
26 Eccleston Street
London SW1W 9PY
http://www.personcare.org

A CIP catalogue record for this book is available from the British
Library

ISBN 0-9547977-4-4

The recommendations in this book are not intended to
replace or conflict with advice given to you by your doctor
or other health care professional. If you have any pre-existing
medical or psychological conditions, or if you are currently
taking medication, you should consult with your doctor
before adopting the suggestions and procedures in this book.

To all Those

who work

for Peace.

Contents

Acknowledgements

A special 'thank you' to Margaret Russo, who has helped turn the original manuscript of this work into the current version and to Anette Foss Ball, for her advice on body movements.

I would like to thank Tina and Alberto Corsi of Borgo la Poggerina, la Romita (Tavarnelle Val di Pesa, Firenze) for the exquisite hospitality in their enchanting house.

"We can harness the energy of the winds,

the seas, the sun.

But the day man learns to harness the energy of love,

That will be as important as the discovery of fire."

Teilhard de Chardin

Introduction

I have been seeing people in distress for the past fifteen years and, during the course of the first nine years, I have employed different approaches to help them overcome their issues: from hypnosis to Jungian analysis, and from humanistic counselling to cognitive-behaviour therapies (i.e. CBT, REBT, Multimodal Therapy).

The application of the above models did not allow me to embrace the whole person though. It was easy to identify archetypes, symptoms, thought patterns and behaviours, but I could as easily lose touch with the very entities who were originating them – the real persons sitting in front of me!

To remedy that, in January 2000, I created a new holistic approach whose practical application consisted of a 15-step person care process which addressed the person's four components (physical sensations, feelings, thoughts and behaviours), three dimensions (intrapersonal, personal and interpersonal), and three time-perspectives (past, present and future).

I originally called my approach Phemiology and referred to its 15-step programme as Phemiological Person Care (PPC), but later renamed it Integrated Person Care. As a result, its application became the IPC process.

Addressing persons' issues by adopting my 15-step person care programme has given me considerable professional satisfaction. However, at the beginning of last year I felt that there still was something missing: my model was *only* a talking cure and I was not working with people's bodies.

I have always believed that human beings are a unity of mindbodyspirit and have personally experienced the benefits of practices like yoga, tai chi, reiki and shiatsu.

It was now comforting to read how world-famous psychiatrists and leading experts in their field started talking and writing openly about the value and usefulness of bodywork.

As Servan-Schreiber observed: *"Neuroscience research has shown clearly that the basic disorders involving depression, stress and anxiety are all related to the functioning of our emotional brain, which we mostly do not understand and look after badly. The same research explains why concentrating on the body can be so effective. Besides producing emotions, the limbic system is also intimately linked with our major metabolic systems – the heart, the guts, the hormones and the immune system. There is constant two-way traffic, with messages coming up about what is going on in the body and messages going out to ensure a smooth working of the whole...This new picture explains why working with the body can be more effective than psychotherapeutic talking cures – the links between the emotional brain and the body are denser and faster than those between the emotional brain and the cortex."* (1)

Bessel van der Kolk also noted how:

"The imprint of trauma is the imprint on people's senses, on people's sensory systems. That becomes particularly important because these sensations stay in people's memory banks and stay unprocessed. If you do effective trauma processing, the individual smells, sounds, images and physical impressions of the trauma slowly disappear over time and that is something that doesn't happen with talking. It happens by working with people's bodily states. When a person experiences trauma, they become highly aroused and, for a period of time, lose their capacity for self-regulation. Parts of the frontal lobe that deal with the capacity to plan, to rationalise, to inhibit inappropriate behaviour – and specifically one area associated with speech – are shown to shut down. People who have experienced trauma need to feel safe in their bodies again. It's via the awareness of deep bodily experience that people can begin to move around the way they feel." (2)

So now my new challenge became connecting and integrating my person care programme with a suitable bodywork practice.

I reviewed all the main bodywork practices being applied at that time and found them all interesting and stimulating. However, they were either too rigid or too floppy, and none of them was providing an integration of gentle body movement and psychological work.

It was then that I decided to create a new practice which would address the whole person by including both bodywork and psychological techniques.

This is how Peaceflow comes about. Since May 2005, its practice has given me peace and joy.

I would now like to share this marvellous experience with you.

Casa Bel Canto
Borgo la Poggerina ~ La Romita
Tavarnelle Val di Pesa (Firenze)
August 2006

Chapter 1
First Element: Presence

"If your compassion does not include yourself, it is incomplete."
Buddha (1)

First step
What is Peaceflow?

With words we may say everything and the opposite of everything, but our body never lies.

We are already aware of the benefits of including a regular exercise routine in our life. We would like to add here that there are other good reasons to make more use of our body.

When we exercise – as well as when we engage in creative activities or when we dream – we activate the right hemisphere of our brain and this allows a beneficial discharge of the excess energy which we tend to accumulate in the left hemisphere during the day.

Focusing on our body also helps us switch off those worries and negative thoughts that we constantly build up in the left hemisphere.

We no longer live in dark cold caves thanks, also, to our innate dynamism: healthy humans don't stand still!

When we feel down and depressed, we tend to reduce considerably our movements and withdraw from social contacts. In such cases, going to the gym or simply going out may feel too much like hard work.

Reconnecting with our body, through gentle bodywork and touch, can help us reverse this downward spiral gradually and comfortably.

There is no such thing as different 'selves' inhabiting our body: a human being is a unity of mindbodyspirit: different components or elements are only the diverse facets by which we perceive who we are.

Movement is change, and change is what we are looking for when we experience distress.

By 'change' we do not mean that there is necessarily something wrong with us: to the contrary, we acknowledge that we are perfectly functioning integrated systems, which would, most of the time, only benefit from assuming a different 'position' towards ourselves and our physical and social environment.

Research carried out at the Royal Hallamshire Hospital in Sheffield (UK), the US National Institute of Health and Harvard's Women's Health Watch on the regular practice of Tai chi, have already shown that gentle body work slows the heart rate and lowers blood pressure in heart attack victims. Moreover, it is effective against arthritis, bone loss and ageing and has a positive effect on diabetes, lower back pain and depression.

Peaceflow is the IPC way of gently moving our body and consists of a number of sequences specifically designed to help us reconnect with the Life forces within, as well as to enhance our overall physical well-being.

Peaceflow is different from traditional forms of gym exercises or practices like Tai chi because:

- it is easy to learn;

- it is easy to remember the movements;

- everybody can practise it, regardless of their age, shape and how fit they are;

- movements are not set in stone but allow for personal variations;

- it is relaxing and pleasurable, unlike the stressful efforts so often associated with gym exercises;

- it frees us from the *curse of the mirror*, that is we can forget about how we look and focus purely on our well-being;

- it provides simple psychological tools which are beautifully integrated into the gentle body movements' sequences.

Presence

Second step
Welcome to yourself!

The main purpose of Integrated Person Care, in general, and of Peaceflow, in particular, is to widen your horizon and help you reconnect with the Life forces which are present, within and around you (i.e. the power of your breathing, the energy of your heart beating, the warmth of the sun, the might of Mother Nature).

Primarily this is a process which asks for first-hand experience of the points being introduced.

As a result, the fifteen steps of Peaceflow are much more brief than the fifteen steps of Integrated Person Care programme: their goal is to show you signposts of how to get to arrive at a number of paths, which only you can follow.

'Being in control' is what most of you want, in order to be able to manage life's events and pursue your objectives.

However, 'being in control' is a condition (or a state of mind, if you wish), which is irreconcilable with the authentic nature of a human being.

We are wonderfully complex, integrated and intelligent systems, but, at the same time, we are limited and fragile.

Therefore, what we would better look for is not 'being in control' but 'being present to ourselves' – that is, living in a state of awareness.

We cannot control the ever-changing flow of life and life's events, but we can be fully aware of them.

As a result, we can, on the one hand, fully enjoy peace and happiness, for the warmth they give to our life; while, on the other, we can fully embrace sadness and distress, for the growing and learning which they bring about.

The next steps will show you techniques and movements which will help you be 'present to yourself' not only when you practise them, but also, in time, for longer parts of the day.

Presence

Third step
The journey within

The Seven Doors practice.

This practice will ask you to go through seven doors. I would recommend that you go through one door per day.

This way, you will be able to memorise the correct sequence of the doors – given that you will be adding just one door at a time, every day, until you reach and go through the seventh – and you will also allow yourself the space to fully explore each room and become aware of your presence there.

Some continue practising by adding one door at a time even when they have memorised the whole sequence: this gives them a sense of self-care, because the seven doors cover each day of the week. Others prefer going through the seven doors every time they practice.

Sit somewhere comfortably, or lay down in bed, if you wish. Close your eyes and slow down your breathing.

When you feel calm and relaxed, begin the practice by following the steps indicated below.

See yourself walking in a beautiful place: it could be a sea resort, somewhere in the country or in the mountains;

At some point, you see a path leading to a house (naturally, the house will reflect the place you are in);

Walk towards the house and reach its main entrance.

Now, you notice that there is writing on the door (the writing could be engraved, painted or tiled). The writing on this **first door** says: "**compassion**".

You know that compassion means 'kindness', 'consideration' and 'care', so when you enter the house through the compassion door, you want to visualise a room where you can feel kind, considerate and caring, first, towards yourself, then, towards others.

The room's layout, furnishing and lighting is entirely up to you, as long as it all makes you feel compassionate.

Once you have allowed enough time to connect with compassion, visualise a second door and make your way towards it;

The writing on the **second door** says: "**sadness**".

You enter this room and you do exactly as you have done in the first room, only now you are connecting with sadness.

This does not mean to 'understand' or 'analyse' your sadness, all you want to do is to 'look for' your sadness and, if you find it, you just 'observe' it and give it a 'home' (i.e. the sadness room's layout, furnishing and lighting).

Naturally, if you don't find it, at this moment in time, you just visualise the third door and come close to it;

The writing on the **third door** says: "**emptiness**".

Here, you would like to create a place where silence reigns: nothing else matters, nothing was, is, or will ever be.

Just find an empty place within you and gradually expand it, until you feel completely empty.

The Roman Emperor and philosopher, Marcus Aurelius, used to say: "If you want to live well, you want to learn to die, every day."

Create emptiness and let yourself go into the sea of nothingness.

As it happens to the seed sown in the earth, that is 'born' and begins its growth in the humid dark of fertile soil, so this room will mother your next step: the rebirth of your inspiration.

The writing on the **fourth door** says: "**inspiration**".

Here, you want to feel inspired: connect with something or somebody that inspires you.

It could be anything: the sunset, the sea, a mountain's peak, a painting, a writer, a sportsman, a musician or an actor.

The writing on the **fifth door** says: "**forgiveness**".

You do exactly as you have done before. Please note that to forgive does not mean to condone: forgiveness means letting go of your own suffering, which is a burden you carry around; to condone means to excuse or to reconcile.

You are perfectly entitled to forgive – something or somebody – without having to justify, excuse or reconcile with them.

Forgiving gives you balance and peace, and frees lots of energy, which can be used in more creative or productive ways.

At the same time, forgiving makes of you a more pleasant person to be around. So, in the end, it works beautifully for your intrapersonal, personal and interpersonal dimensions.

The writing on the **sixth door** says: "**peace**".

You do as you have done before. Again, always start with yourself: first, make peace with you, and, only then, make peace with others.

The writing on the **seventh door** says: "**love**".

As you have done in the 'peace' room, begin first by loving yourself, and only then move your feelings of warmth and affection towards others.

Choose a place in your body where you most feel the warmth of love, and gradually expand this wonderful feeling all over your body: allow the transforming and healing power of love into your life, surrendering completely to it.

Presence

Fourth step
Warm up

Moving your body.

Internal balance and strength are not qualities inherited from birth. They come from aligning the body, opening the joints and relaxing the muscles.

The Chinese call our vital energy 'Chi' – 'Ki' in Japanese. We will simply refer to it as 'energy'.

Peaceflow movements are specifically designed to help you rebalance the flow of energy through your body.

Having said that, please bear in mind that their principal focus still remains the very centre of energy in your body.

The Chinese call this 'Tan T'ien' and the Japanese 'Hara', and is located approximately 1 and ½ inches below the navel.

From now on, we will call our energy centre simply 'the centre'.

All Peaceflow movements will be more effective if you feel your centre and feel that, with your breathing, you are spreading the flow of energy from your centre to each part of your body.

So, when you breathe in, first make sure that the air reaches your lower abdomen, next visualise that it touches your centre, and then, that it spreads to each part of your body before you breathe out.

Warm up.

The following nine sets of warm up movements will help you prepare for the seven sequences of Peaceflow.

Please note that you are required to carry out each movement **very slowly**, **gently** and **gradually**: this will ensure your full enjoyment as well as the beneficial outcome of your practice.

Fast, sudden and abrupt movements can cause discomfort or injury, especially if you haven't exercised for some time.

1. Assume the starting position.

Eastern medicine views the body as a musical instrument, which needs to be tuned to fulfil its potential and generate sound.

We tune our body by assuming a correct posture.

To do this, follow the simple steps below:

   a) stand, as if the head is suspended from the ceiling;

   b) bend the knees slightly to lower the centre of gravity and stretch the spine;

   c) sink the shoulders to release the tension built there;

   d) breathe deep into the abdomen.

Make sure that your knees do not go beyond the imaginary perpendicular line which aligns them with the tips of your toes.

Once you are satisfied that your posture is correct, close your eyes and take a few deep breaths.

Breathe slowly, gently and deeply (exactly in this order), in this starting position for 3 or 4 minutes.

2. Bring your knees back to the normal standing posture and then bend them to reassume the starting position a few times.

3. Bend your right leg forward, while the left leg goes slightly backward. Make sure that you feel balanced and comfortable.

Move your weight forward onto the right leg and backward onto the left leg a few times, as in a 'rubber band-like' rolling movement.

Reverse the movement with the left leg bent forward and the right backward.

4. Go back to the starting position and, while keeping your feet firmly on the ground, begin undulating your body – as if your legs and spine were a sailing-vessel mast – first to the right and to the left, next forward and backward, and then, clockwise and anticlockwise.

5. Same movements as above, this time by undulating your pelvis.

6. Twist your pelvis, first to the right, and then to the left, a few times.

Make sure that your arms are totally relaxed: they will move only as a result of the hips' turning.

7. Your arms move forward, as if you were gently pushing something away, and return to your side.

Do this a few times, then reverse by moving your arms backwards.

8. Tilt your neck, first forward and backward, next to the right and to the left, and then, clockwise and anticlockwise.

9. Complete this warm up sequence by slightly bouncing, up and down, as if your whole body – from the tips of your toes to the top of your head – were a rubber-band.

Feel your body loose as if you were a puppet on a string.

It is important that you carry out the warm up above before beginning the practice of each of the seven Peaceflow sequences you will find in the forthcoming steps.

Presence

Fifth step
The sailing-vessel

First sequence: the sailing-vessel,

This sequence consists of three exercises: the wave, the circle and the sailing-vessel.

The wave.

> ➤ Extend your arms, parallel and with palms facing down.

> ➤ Rotate both arms clockwise 90 degrees – that is, your arms are in line with your body with your palms facing left.

> ➤ Move your arms to the left, and then, first, bring your left hand down while the right goes up, and next, with your palms facing right, move your arms to the right.

> ➤ Bring your right arm down and the left up, with palms facing left, and restart the entire movement again.

It is as if you are drawing a wave with your arms, gently pushing something away, and your body is gently following your arms movements with a slight bending motion of your legs and torso.

The circle.

Stretch both arms to one side and move them in a circular motion, initially, a few times clockwise, then, anticlockwise.

It is as if, with your circular movements, you are drawing a circle which goes from as far as your arms can stretch to your right, to your left and above your head.

Please make sure that you begin with slow and gentle movements. Only when you feel happy and comfortable with the exercise, may you increase the speed.

Always make sure, if you increase the speed, to do it gradually, both when you speed up and when you slow down.

Our heart does not like sudden 'start and stop' movements, which is why you want to warm up and be fit before playing games like tennis.

The sailing-vessel.

- ➤ Keep your feet firmly rooted to the ground and begin gently undulating your body, initially forward and backward.

- ➤ Then, to the right and to the left.

- ➤ Next, in a circular way, both clockwise and anticlockwise.

- ➤ Finally, carry on by allowing your body to lead you in any direction it may wish to go.

I would suggest you first familiarise yourself with the first two movements, and then, you move to the latter.

This exercise is called the sailing-vessel, because, to make the most of it, you would like to imagine that you are a vessel: your feet are the deck and your body is the mast.

Your movements come as a result of sea waves. These waves generate a gentle, slow and powerful rolling that you simply follow with your mast.

You may wish to practise this exercise with your eyes closed: this way you can visualise wonderful coastlines and turquoise seas, swimming dolphins or flying birds, as well as 'feel' a gentle breeze caressing your face.

To complete this exercise, first, make sure that your eyes are closed and assume a true 'mast position', by fully extending your arms: you are now feeling the energy of the sun and the wind, and you are receiving it through your palms.

Next, first extend your arms to the sky, palms facing up, and then, bring both hands to your centre (just below your navel), palms facing in, and keep them there for a few moments.

Finally, slowly open your eyes.

Chapter 2

Second Element: Energy

"You are the light of the world.
Let your light shine before men."

Jesus (1)

"The more fully we give our energy,
the more it returns to us."

Buddha (2)

Sixth step
Going with the flow

As physical movement enhances a person's capacity for movement of thought, so the awareness of our flow of energy can help us reconnect with our inner vital resources which originate from our bond with the natural world.

What do we mean by 'energy'? We are certainly not referring to some sort of ethereal and mysterious entity, dreamed by an ascetic master thousands of years ago: we can feel and touch our internal energy any time we want!

Just place your hand on your wrist, what do you feel? The sensation of warmth coming from this contact is the result of the vital activity of billions of cells in your body: you are alive thanks to their energy, which is yours to dispose of.

Recent research has shown how each human cell is a wonderful autonomous system on its own, while, at the same time, being perfectly integrated with its environment, that is, our entire body.

Energy flows through our body thanks to the blood circulation, the lymphatic system and nerve endings which connect each square millimetre of our body.

Traditional Chinese medicine has, for thousands of years, focused its attention on how important it is to look after and, possibly enhance, the internal flow of energy throughout our body, in order to prevent and cure a number of illnesses.

Practices now fully recognised in Western societies, such as acupuncture, yoga, shiatsu and tai chi, are all based on the Eastern assumption that illnesses and discomfort arise when the flow of energy is either blocked or in excess in some specific areas of our body.

Centuries of practical work on energy and the experiential awareness acquired have indicated to Eastern practitioners that there are a number of energy lines which cover the full length of our body: we call them meridians.

The correct practice of appropriate movements – like the ones indicated in our Peaceflow steps – result in a free flow of energy that can be greatly beneficial for our well-being.

Back to Life Technique.

Find an appropriate quiet place, at home or at the office. Lower or switch off the light, if you can, and make yourself comfortable.

It would be useful to listen to a recording of your voice reading very slowly the paragraphs below: you could easily do that with a memo or tape recorder, some mobile phones can also perform this function nowadays. Also, please make sure that you stop for a moment (i.e. 20 to 30 seconds) at the pauses in the text as indicated by '…'.

"Focus your attention on your body. How does it feel? Close your eyes. Take a few slow and deep breaths. Push the air down to your abdomen (= your centre), become aware of your breathing ... of the air coming in your body ... and the air going out ... feel this flow.

Now, feel your heart beat ... listen to it ... feel it ... and connect with its flow.

You know nothing ... you are nothing ... your body keeps you alive ... your lungs breathe ... your heart beats ... the blood flows throughout your body ... billions of nerve cells make you feel cold or warmth ... your body knows what to do ... you know nothing ... only your body ... in its infinite wisdom ... knows.

Your body is alive ... there are billions of living cells in your body ... there are billions of living cells in a flower ... you are like a flower ... what kind of flower are you? ... what is your colour? ... what is your smell? ... there are billions of cells in a tree ... you are like a tree ... what kind of tree are you? ... what kind of branches do you have? ... little birds are nesting on your tree ... what birds are they? ... what is their colour?

You are alive ... everything around you is alive ... you are one of billions of living creatures on Earth ... you are filled with Life ... they are filled with Life ... Life is here ... Life is everywhere ... Life is constant change ... Life is flow ... feel the flow of your breath ... feel your heart beat ... feel the quiet and silence around you ... take a few deep breaths ... and only when you are ready ... slowly and gently ... open your eyes."

Energy

Seventh step
The sage's hug

Second sequence: the sage's hug.

This sequence consists of three exercises: the wave, the circle (which you have learnt in the first sequence) and the sage's hug.

The sage's hug.

> ➢ Close your eyes and imagine yourself as a sage. Then, stretch your arms forward, just like you are hugging something or somebody.

> ➢ Visualise that with your hug you are embracing a wonderful tree, an unknown beautiful woman, or a handsome man, or something or somebody you know. You are receiving a great deal of energy from this embrace.

> ➢ Stay in that position for 3 to 4 minutes, while continuing to breathe slowly, gently and deeply. Then, relax your arms for a couple of minutes.

> ➢ Now visualise that you are hugging something or somebody else. This time you are giving them your energy.

> ➢ At some point, you will feel a tingling in your fingers. When this happens, first extend your arms to the sky, palms facing up, and then, bring both hands to our centre (just below your navel), palms facing in, and keep them there for a few moments.

> ➢ Finally, slowly open your eyes.

With practice, you will be able to keep your arms stretched for a longer period of time.

However, as with all our bodywork, we are not looking for quantity but, rather, quality: we would like to enjoy Peaceflow movements, from start to finish – that's our golden rule – and we complete them when we feel we are happy to end them.

It is better to carry out our movements for shorter periods of time and to enjoy the activity, than to overdo them and feel discomfort in the process: what makes a difference for our well-being is regularity of practice, not excessive and episodic efforts!

Energy

Eighth step
The heron

Third sequence: the heron.

This sequence consists of three exercises: the wave, the circle and the heron. You have learnt how to practise the first two in the first sequence, now let's introduce the third.

The heron.

> ➤ Close your eyes and imagine yourself as a heron in its natural environment: your feet are in the water and the beauty of nature is all around you.

> ➤ Lift your right foot slowly and move it slightly forward with your toes pointing down.

> ➤ Your foot is very close to the ground, but is not touching it.

> ➤ Then, slowly lift your right knee and stop before your leg reaches the 90 degree angle.

> ➤ Slowly put your right leg down and do the same with your left.

> ➤ Next, make a few steps in any direction you like by moving your legs, one by one, according to the above indicated movement: that is, your body weight is first on one leg and then on the other. So, you extend one foot, then lift the leg, and finally, make your step. Then, you do the same with the other leg.

Now, stand with both feet on the ground and your eyes closed.

➤ When you are ready, spread your wings, by lifting your arms, and shake them gently to shed the water.

➤ Feel your wings drying in the warm sun.

To complete this exercise, first extend your arms to the sky, palms facing up, and then, bring both hands to your centre (just below your navel), palms facing in, and keep them there for a few moments.

Finally, slowly open your eyes.

Energy

Ninth step
The hermit's blessing

Fourth sequence: the hermit's blessing.

This sequence consists of three exercises: the wave, the circle and the hermit's blessing. You have learnt how to practise the first two in the first sequence, now let's introduce the third.

The hermit's blessing.

> ➢ Close your eyes and imagine yourself as a hermit who lives on a mountain.

> ➢ You are standing in the open and you can see a beautiful scenery surrounding you: warm sun, blue sky, mountains, a valley below and a village in the distance.

> ➢ Become fully aware of the beauty of the nature around you.

> ➢ Raise your forearms, keeping your elbows by your side, palms facing up – in a thanksgiving posture.

> ➢ Feel at peace with yourself and nature. Allow the energy of nature to enter your body through your palms and let it spread all over you.

> ➢ Count the blessings in your life.

> ➢ Extend – without stretching – your arms forward and direct your palms towards the valley below.

➢ Direct your energy and your blessing toward the valley below and its people.

To complete the exercise, first extend your arms to the sky, palms facing up, and then, bring both hands to your centre (just below your navel), palms facing in, and keep them there for a few moments.

Finally, slowly open your eyes.

Chapter 3

Third Element: Communicative heart

"We make a living by what we get,
but we make a life by what we give."

Winston Churchill

"Love in the past is only a memory.
Love in the future is a fantasy.
Only here and now can we truly love."

Buddha

Tenth step
Open up your heart

Too much thinking poisons our body with deadlines, criticism, assessments, higher goals and worries.

From time to time, it is very beneficial to disconnect from our rational mind and stop interfering with our inner vital processes.

Switch off the constant noise of your environment and make a bit of time and space to allow silence to embrace you and help you reconnect with Life.

Only when we feel connected with Life, are we able to fully experience the flow of energy that nourishes and supports us and all the living creatures on Earth.

Only then, are we capable of connecting with the sadness and the joy which is within and around us. Only then, can we experience peace.

Thus, opening up our heart is not a specific – though enlightened – action, but rather, a life-long experiential process where we open ourselves up to the depths of our conscience and to the breadth of our world.

One way to do this is to practise the 'connecting with love' technique indicated below.

Communicative heart

Eleventh step
Giving and receiving love

We are not even attempting here a definition of 'love': we may all have our own ideas of what love is, of how we fall in love or fall out of it. For some love is an everlasting feeling, for others a transient emotion.

In our person care programme, we view love as yet another life force: a powerful and, at times, overwhelming force which can trigger a range of emotional responses, as well as unpredictable choices and behaviours.

Love can change one's life, love has the power to transform who we are and what we do with our life.

We can make a beneficial use of this force by connecting with it and utilising its energy to direct light into our deepest and darkest inner places; to warmly embrace our sadness; to motivate us to break our self-inflicted isolation and grant ourselves permission to go out there and live life.

When you feel low or depressed; when you are not quite sure whether you are in an appropriate place; when you don't feel comfortable with your partner, in particular, or with your social life, in general, you may find it useful to practise the following two activities: 'connecting with love' and 'the love pie'.

Connecting with love.

You will find it easy to remember this exercise because it is divided into four consecutive steps each beginning with the four letters making up the word 'love'.

You may also wish to listen to your own recording of the steps, as in the 'back to Life' technique. In this case, please allow a pause between each step to ensure you have enough time to carry out the indicated tasks.

Find a quiet place. Switch off your mobile phone and other sources of noise.

Make yourself comfortable and close your eyes. Take a few deep and slow breaths and begin the exercise.

Look inside yourself: go and find your sadness or issue. Find the place in your body where you most feel it.

Observe your sadness or issue. Do not analyse, do not ask questions: just observe it for what and how it is.

Visualise love as light. What is the colour of your love? Find the place in your body where you most feel it.

Experience the warmth that is now, gently and gradually, spreading from the place where you most feel love to the rest of your body.

When you reach the place where you most feel your sadness – or issue – let the light of love go around it, like a warm embrace, until you see and feel that your place of sadness is completely embraced by the light of love.

Let this light penetrate the place of sadness and let it spread within, until this place is completely filled with the light of love.

Observe this. Feel this. Feel the warmth of the light of love which has now spread all over your body.

Stay there, connected with this feeling, calm and at peace, for a couple of minutes. Then, slowly open your eyes.

The love pie.

On day one, begin by writing down the different ways in which somebody – not you in particular – may give and receive love: make one list for giving and one for receiving (your lists may have items like: mother's love, friend's love, etc.).

Once the two lists are completed, number the items in order of how valuable you think they are.

Then, draw a couple of circles (pies), slice them up by inserting the items from your lists, and you may also reflect the value you have attached to your items by drawing a bigger slice for the more valuable items and a smaller slice for the others.

The next day, write down two lists including the different ways in which you are giving and receiving love.

You now proceed as with day one, by placing your items, first, in order of how much you value them, and then, by drawing a couple of pies which will graphically represent your lists.

The third day, you place the two different sets of pies together and observe them: what do they show?

Don't analyse, just observe what you see. Are you a giver or a receiver?

Are you directing your energy mostly towards one or two persons (i.e. your pie shows big slices)? How is the receiving?

This observation may offer you an awareness of your current situation which you might have missed so far, especially if some major unbalance comes up: this may help your motivation in introduce changes in the way you address your personal and social life.

In my professional experience, I have found that people find this activity very stimulating, and often, some interesting points tend to come up.

Communicative heart

Twelfth step
The dancer

Fifth sequence: the dancer.

This sequence consists of three exercises: the wave, the circle and the dancer. You have learnt how to practise the first two in the first sequence, now let's introduce the third.

The dancer.

➤ Close your eyes and start a free-flowing dance.

➤ You may visualise that you are dancing on your own or with somebody else.

➤ As you take each step, you want to feel the pleasure of free movement and, at the same time, feel fully balanced.

➤ Next, make a few steps, one leg at a time, as in the heron's exercise.

➤ Now, return to free-flowing movements and make a few joyful steps.

To complete the exercise, extend your arms to the sky, palms facing up, like they were antennae receiving the world's energy and converting it into an exhilarating feeling of joy.

Next, guide your hands to a particular place in your body which may benefit from warmth and comfort.

Then, bring both hands to your centre (just below your navel), palms facing in, and keep them there for a few moments. Finally, slowly open your eyes.

Communicative heart

Thirteenth step
The tree

Sixth sequence: the tree.

This sequence consists of three exercises: the wave, the circle and the tree. You have learnt how to practise the first two in the first sequence, now let's introduce the third.

The tree.

> ➢ Close your eyes and imagine yourself as a tree.

> ➢ Feel your centre sinking, first, down to the ground, and then, below the ground, as if you were a tree becoming fully aware of its roots.

> ➢ Feel the air flowing in and out of your system.

> ➢ Feel the blood flow.

> ➢ Feel the energy coming from your roots and let this energy flow all the way up, allowing it to reach the top of your trunk (= your head) and your main branches (= your extended arms).

> ➢ Now, bring your focus back to your centre and feel your body strong and alive.

> ➢ Extend your arms slightly and comfortably as if they were tree branches.

> Feel that Life is making use of them: birds stop by chirping joyfully and little creatures take refuge from the heat under their shade. You have been there since the beginning of time and you will always be there to provide for the universe's little ones: the ones in search of safety and comfort.

> Feel the energy at the very end of your branches (= your hands).

Next, guide your hands to a particular place in your body which may benefit from warmth and comfort.

To complete this exercise, first extend your arms to the sky, palms facing up, and then, bring both hands to your centre (just below your navel), palms facing in, and keep them there for a few moments.

Finally, slowly open your eyes.

Communicative heart

Fourteenth step
The eagle's flight

Seventh sequence: the eagle's flight.

This sequence consists of three exercises: the wave, the circle and the eagle's flight. You have learnt how to practise the first two in the first sequence, now let's introduce the third.

The eagle's flight.

> ➢ Close your eyes and imagine yourself as an eagle perched on a tree branch.

> ➢ You are in a beautiful place up in the mountains and the view from your standpoint is breathtaking.

> ➢ Slowly lift your heels and bring them back to the ground. Do this twice.

> ➢ Spread your 'wings' and move them as if you were flying away.

> ➢ Enjoy the stunning view and the wonderful flight by extending your arms comfortably and making slow and harmonious movements.

> ➢ Feel light, weightless.

> ➢ Feel above everything you see. You are so high up nothing can touch you and nobody can reach you.

- You breathe the purest air and feel the wind on your face.

- Silence is all around: a profound peace possesses you now.

- You are flying and your wings are moving, but you are perfectly still within.

- Now, find a place where to rest.

- Next, guide your hands to a particular place in your body which may benefit from warmth and comfort.

- Then, first extend your arms to the sky, palms facing up, and then, bring them down and move both hands to your centre (just below your navel), palms facing in, and keep them there for a few moments.

- Finally, slowly open your eyes.

Communicative heart

Fifteenth step
The gentle touch

Peaceflow does not only benefit our movement of thought and our flow of energy, it can also help improve our ability to love by removing the blocks that we have placed between us and our personal and social environment.

As Vincenzo Rossi observes: *"If my ability to love is 'ten' and I live only a 'three', out of my potential of ten, given the fundamental unity of mindbodyspirit, my body will only show 30% of all those movements which reflect care, love, affection and joy for life. Therefore, by moving my body beyond that 30%, I evoke a change, at all levels of my being, which will help my personal growth as well as my relating to others." (1)*

Getting in touch with your body.

Touch can express empathy, care and affection much more than any words can ever do! Sadly, our technologically advanced Western societies have lost the value and meaning of touch and the Western approach to medical and psychological care duly reflects the collective sexual repression and lack of humanity in our societies.

The sale of all sorts of pornographic material is allowed, and brothels are either legalised, or tolerated, pretty much everywhere, but health practitioners have to be very careful during a consultation to avoid any form of physical contact.

Patients are touched only when a physical examination is deemed appropriate, other than that, no physician – let alone a psychologist – would ever dream of establishing a connection with the person in their care by gently shaking their hands, touching their shoulders or their cheek.

One of the reasons behind the growing popularity – and therapeutic success – of complementary approaches to care such as acupuncture, shiatsu, reflexology, Alexander's techniques, etc., is precisely the direct contact established between the practitioner and the person.

As the Master of Zen Shiatsu, Tetsugen Serra, observes: *"the fundamental experience for the human being, regardless of their ethnic origin or social status, is not the verbal communication, but, rather, the direct physical connection." (2)*

Naturally, I am not suggesting that health practitioners should start hugging and kissing the persons in their care: what I mean is that, at the appropriate time, a gentle touch on the hand, arm or shoulder, can help a person much more than half an hour of mere words.

After all, if we have at heart the well-being of the persons in our care – as it should be – it would be useful to consider how inappropriate verbal remarks can offend or harm a person much more than any gentle touch could!

In the end, it is down to the professionalism and the sense of responsibility of the practitioner whether we use verbal communication, body language or bodywork.

When we apply a gentle touch to our body – and some areas are more sensitive than others – we release soothing chemicals such as serotonin, which can help us feel more at ease with ourselves, more balanced internally and more comfortable with our physical and social environment.

We would like you to experience the above by practising the exercise below.

The gentle touch.

Wear something loose and comfortable, lie down, close your eyes, take a few slow and deep breaths and then, start the following sequence of gentle touches:

> ➤ begin with your abdomen; make sure that your hand is warm (you can do that by rubbing your hands together) and place your hand directly on your abdomen; now, slowly and gently rub your abdomen, with a circular motion that has, as the centre, your navel, with a radius of approx. 1 and ½ inches;

> ➤ move up to your face; locate your 'third eye', which is a small cavity between your eyes and just above them; using the tip of your finger, rub it, slowly and gently with a circular motion;

> ➤ place use fingertips on your temples; hold them there, still, for a moment; then begin massaging your temples, slowly and gently, in a circular motion. Please do this very gently, as our temples are a very sensitive part of our system;

> ➤ place both hands on your mastoids, which are the two conical prominences on our temporal bones, just behind our ears; begin massaging them, gently and slowly, with a circular motion;

> ➤ place the tip of one of your fingers on one eye-lid and begin rubbing it, very softly, in a circular motion; do the same with the other eye-lid;

> ➤ place the tip of one of your fingers, from each hand, on either side of your mouth (i.e. the right hand's finger on the right side of your mouth, and likewise for the left. Begin massaging this area, with a synchronic and gentle circular motion;

> ➤

➤ move down to your chin; place the tip of one of your fingers on it and start massaging it, slowly and gently, with a circular motion;

➤ move down to your abdomen and repeat point a), only now you are, first, massaging it, and, then, you complete the exercise by gently rubbing it a few times, always in a circular motion.

Chapter 4

Notes for the journey ahead

"The only thing necessary for the triumph of evil is for good men to do nothing."

Edmund Burke

"It is man who makes truth great, not truth which makes man great."

Confucius

The 21st century Renaissance.

Peaceflow and the Integrated Person Care programme are part of a wider cultural framework which I have called 'the 21st century Renaissance'.

The 15th century Renaissance consisted of a revival in arts and literature which originated in Florence: its main aspiration consisted of a rediscovery of the human being and of the natural world.

After centuries of bowing to external and intangible forces, human beings were finally seen as their own masters and educators.

People and environments were represented as they really were, rather than as they should be: pure geniuses like Brunelleschi, Masaccio and Donatello paved the way for the extraordinary accomplishments of Raffaello and Leonardo da Vinci.

The 21st century Renaissance encourages all of us to create the conditions for a reawakening of our connection both with the healing power of the life forces **within** us – the 'biological' (i.e. breathing and energy) as well as the 'creative' ones (i.e. arts and music) – and **around** us (the natural world and fellow human beings).

It also invites us to open up our hearts and share this awareness with each other.

Our message for you is:

"Join the 21st century Renaissance. Start giving in to your spontaneity and creativity. Begin taking care of yourself. Now!"

Getting in touch.

Our school offers one-to-one consultations, classes and workshops in IPC and Peaceflow, on a weekly or intensive basis, both in London and abroad (currently in Tuscany).

I would really appreciate your comments on this little guide. Your feedback and criticism can contribute to helping other sufferers, carers or practitioners. I will use them both in my professional practice and in my next publications. Please forward your opinions to:

Tommaso Palumbo
School of Integrated Person Care
26 Eccleston Street
London ~ SW1W 9PY
Telephone: 0044 020 7881 0601
Email: info@peaceflow.org
Website: http://www.peaceflow.org

Training in Peaceflow.

The practice of Peaceflow is open to everybody, though I would still recommend that you attended some Peaceflow classes before practising on your own.

Training in Peaceflow is also open to everybody. You may become a Master Practitioner of Peaceflow in six months of intensive training and you will be granted authorisation to set up your own Peaceflow School where you could deliver classes and training.

Please note that Peaceflow is a trademark. Unauthorised use of its name and working model will be liable to prosecution in the competent courts of law.

For further information on our School of Integrated Person Care and our training please visit our website:
http://www.peaceflow.org

Notes

Introduction

1. Servan-Schreiber in Burne (2004)
2. Van der Kolk in Pointon (2204), p. 11

1. First Element: Presence

1. Buddha in Kornfield (1994), p. 47

2. Second Element: Energy

1. Jesus in Matthew 4:14-16
2. Buddha in Kornfield (1994), p. 37

3. Third Element: Communicative Heart

1. Rossi, V. (2004)
2. Serra, T. (2005)

Bibliography

Books

Assagioli, R. (1971) *Psychosynthesis*, New York: Viking.

Beck, A. T. (1991) *Cognitive Therapy and the Emotional Disorders*, London: Penguin Books.

Bellino, F. (1988) *Etica della Solidarieta` e Societa` Complessa (Ethics of Solidarity and Complex Society)*, Bari: Levante.

Bettelheim, B. (1982) *Freud and Man's Soul*, London: Penguin Books.

Borrelli, S. E. & Palumbo, T. (2004) *Italy,* in Malley-Morrison K. (ed.) *International Perspectives on Family Violence and Abuse*, Mahwah (NJ): Lawrence Erlbaum Associates.

De Crescenzo, L. (1983) *Storia della Filosofia Greca – I Presocratici (History of Greek Philosophy, Part 1)*, Milano: Mondadori.

De Crescenzo, L. (1986) *Storia della Filosofia Greca – Da Socrate in poi (History of Greek Philosophy, Part 2)*, Milano: Mondadori.

De Crescenzo, L. (2002) *Storia della Filosofia Medioevale (History of Medieval Philosophy)*, Milano: Mondadori

Dryden, W. (1999) *Rational Emotive Behavioural Counselling in Action*, London: Sage.

Filippani-Ronconi, P. (1994) *Il Buddismo (Buddhism)*, Roma: Newton Compton.

Freud, A. (1993) *Anna Freud: Her Life and Work*, London: Freud Museum Publications.

Freud, S. (1991) *Introductory Lectures on Psychoanalysis*, London: Penguin Books.

Furedi, F. (2004) *Therapy Culture*, London: Routledge.

Goleman, D. (1995) *Emotional Intelligence*, Glasgow: ThorsonsAudio.

Gross, R. D. (1999) Psychology: *The Science of Mind and Behaviour*, London: Hodder & Stoughton.

Hadot, P. (1999) *Philosophy as a Way of Life*, Oxford: Blackwell.

Hirst, B. (2002) *Il riso non cresce sugli alberi (Rice does not grow on trees)*, Milano: La Tartaruga.

Jacobs, M. (2002) *Psychodynamic Counselling in Action*, London: Sage.

Kornfield, J. (1994) *Buddha's Little Instruction Book*, New York: Bantam Books.

Laszlo, E. (1978) in Bellino, F. (1988) *Etica della Solidarieta` e Societa` Complessa (Ethics of Solidarity and Complex Society)*, Bari: Levante.

Lazarus, A. A. (1997) *Brief but Comprehensive Psychotherapy*, New York: Springer.

Lawrence, J. in *The Bathroom Inspiration Book*, Saddle River (NJ): Red-Letter Press.

Lefever, R. (2003) *Eating Disorders*, Nonington (Kent): Promis.

Lerner, M. D. and Sheldon, R. D. *Acute Traumatic Stress Management*, New York: AAETS.

Petronio, G. (1977) *Italia Letteraria (History of Italian Literature)*, Roma: Palumbo.

Pinel, J. P. J. (2003) *Biopsychology*, Boston: Allyn and Bacon.

Rossi, V. (2004) *La via del movimento*, Diagaro di Cesena: Macroedizioni

Serra, T. (2005) *Zen Shiatsu,* Milano: Fabbri

Smail, D. (1993) *The Origins of Unhappiness*, London: Harper Collins.

Smail, D. (1998) *How To Survive Without Psychotherapy*, London: Constable.

Thich Nhat Hanh (1997) in Luchinger, T. *Steps of Mindfulness (video)*, Zurich: Luchinger.

Vinay, M.P. (1973) *Hygiene Mentale (Mental Hygiene)*, St Francois Sherbrooke: Editions Paulines.

Articles, papers and training

Burne, J. (2004) *Can this man cure your depression?* The Independent Review, 17 May 2004.

Canter, D. (2002) *The rise and rise of biobabble*, New Scientist, Vol. 173, issue 2336, 30 March 2002, p. 50.

Davidson, R. (2004) in Huppert, Baylis, Keverne (2004) *The science of well-being*, The Psychologist, Vol. 17, No. 1, p. 7.

Deary, I. (2003) *Ten Things I hate about Intelligence Research*, The Psychologist, Vol. 16, No 10, p. 537.

Fairburn, C. G. and Harrison P. J. (2003) *Eating Disorders*, Lancet 2003; 361: 407-16.

Farley, P. (2004) *The anatomy of despair*, New Scientist, Vol. 182, issue 2445, 01 May 2004, p. 42.

Healy (1998) in Palumbo, T. (1999) *A brief Introduction to Essential Psychology*, London (unpublished paper).

Lanza del Vasto (1975), poet, Christian mystic and non-violent activist, Fellowship Magazine, Sept. 1975.

Lawson, W. (2004) *The Glee Club*, Psychology Today, February 2004, p. 34.

Malley-Morrison, K. (2004) *The Evil of Inaction*, Talk given to graduating MA students, Boston University, 16 May 2004.

Morelli, R. & Zerbini E. (2006) *Training in Anti-stress Bodywork*, Rome: Riza Institute.

Palumbo, T. (1999) *A brief Introduction to Essential Psychology*, CMQ, Vol. X, No. 2 (286), London: GCD.

Pointon, C. (2004) *The future of trauma work*, Counselling and Psychotherapy Journal UK, May 2004, p. 10.

Rowe, D. (2001) *The story of depression*, Counselling and Psychotherapy Journal UK, November 2001, p. 5.

Small, M. F. (2002) *The happy fat*, New Scientist, Vol. 175, issue 2357, 24 August 2002, p. 34.

Thernstrom, M. (2001) *Life Without Pain*, The New York Times Magazine, December 16, 2001, New York.

Van der Kolk, B. A. (2002) *EMDR, consciousness and the body*, Boston: The Trauma Center.

Resources

Books

DesMaisons K. (2001) *Potatoes not Prozac*, London: Simon & Schuster.

Kornfield, J. (1994) *Buddha's Little Instruction Book*, New York: Bantam Books.

Tolle, E. (2005) *The Power of Now,* London: Hodder & Stoughton

Professional Organisations

The British Association for Counselling and Psychotherapy (BACP)
BACP House, 35-37 Albert Street, Rugby, CV21 2SG
Tel: 0870 443 5252 - Website: www.bacp.co.uk

The British Psychological Society (BPS)
St Andrews House, 48 Princess Road East, Leicester LE1 7DR
Tel: 0116 254 9568 - Website: www.bps.org.uk

Other National Organisations

The Eating Disorders Association (EDA)
First Floor, Wensum House, 103 Prince of Wales Road, Norwich NR1 1DW
Tel: 0870 770 3256 – Website: www.edauk.com

The National Centre for Eating Disorders (NCFED)
54 New Road, Esher, Surrey, KT10 9NU
Tel: 01372 469 493 – Website: www.eating-disorders.org.uk